A Librarian is to Read

A Librarian is to Read

by
Betty Vogel

3

Canadian Cataloguing in Publication Data

Vogel, Betty, 1931–
  A librarian is to read

  ISBN 0-88925-877-5

  1. Public libraries - Anecdotes.
  2. Public libraries - Humor. I. Title.
  Z682.5.V64 1988   027.4'02'07   C88-091377-0

© 1988 Betty Vogel

Blue Flower Press
101-309 E. Cordova St.
Vancouver, B.C.
Canada
V6A 1L4

Printed in Canada

To
Edith Fry
and
Virginia Reich

Acknowledgements

About half of the material in this book comes from sources other than myself. I should like to thank my co-workers who have shared their experiences with me. I am particularly indebted to Nancy Dore of Brighton, England, who, in a supreme feat of reference librarianship, quickly retrieved a thirty year old satire from library school days. I also owe a great debt to **Flash**, the newsletter of the Seattle Public Library, which I have unconscionably plagiarized.

PREFACE

While rooting through some old memorabilia, I recently came across this manuscript, which I had written in 1976 while employed by the Seattle Public Library. Although it may appear somewhat dated, I have decided to publish it, as there seems little possibility of convincing any publisher to print any of my tortured autobiographical novels. This may be regarded as a rather ridiculous monument to my ego, or as a contribution to the somewhat meager literature on library humor, depending on your point of view.

There is no mention of computers or AIDS in this book, and, admittedly, some of the attitudes expressed in it may appear to arise from a much more innocent age. Nevertheless, the public library patron, around whom this book revolves, remains eternal. In thousands of libraries around the world they are still passionately pursuing some elusive fact, doing their meticulous and often esoteric research — in short, devoting themselves to some magnificent obsession which gives meaning to their lives.

Next to religion, which Jung regarded as "the world's great psychotherapeutic system", it is the free creative life of the individual which gives most meaning to our lives. And, for most people, where can this be more easily expressed and fulfilled than among the rich resources which most public libraries have to offer?

One criticism which I have occasionally received after printing some of these unpretentious little stories, was that I was "putting down the patron".

However, as a librarian, I feel neither bound by the Hippocratic oath nor the seal of the confessional, which, I believe, are incumbent upon quite other professions. I see no reason why the comments which the patron so eagerly and ingenuously offers must be repressed forever into the subconscious. The immense joy of working in a public library consists in revelling in the vast richness and peculiarity of the human personality, which we are so privileged to observe. If there is an element of tragedy in our patrons' secret passions and obsessions or their frequent lack of comprehension, it is a tragedy shared by us all. It is, in fact, the common lot of the whole, poor, suffering, confused human race.

Betty Vogel
Vancouver, B.C.
Eastertide, 1988

Contents

On Seeking a Viable Alternative to Librarianship

I have always assumed that, after enduring the agony of library school, the least society could do was to provide one with a job. However, now that librarians, along with other professional people, are a drug on the market, this no longer seems to be the case. The more flexible seek a creative alternative — usually opening a pizza parlor — while the inflexible stay at home reading Nietzsche and collecting food stamps.

Once, while in between jobs, I also toyed with the idea of doing something else, and eagerly searched the classified ads in the newspaper. While some jobs seemed obviously unsuitable — e.g., running a Hudson's Bay Company trading post in Inuvik — I was certain that many promising opportunities remained. It was a great shock to discover that, far from being "overqualified," I was quite incapable of doing most of the jobs in the first place.

First, there were the usual ads for jobs requiring domestic skills — dish washing, cooking and housekeeping. Although I occasionally enjoy washing the odd dish at a meditative pace while thinking of something more significant, I can't imagine actually concentrating on it and pursuing it as a career. Being a cook also seemed out of the question. The only dish I have ever successfully mastered is "creamy egg on toast" which comprised the first lesson in our Grade Seven home economics class. (I gave up when confronted by the complexities of blancmange.) The housekeeping jobs seemed scarcely more inviting, although they often had promising openers:

"Luxurious Living in Beautiful Suburban Home! Light housekeeping only, look after eight lovely children! Make 3 meals a day, do dishes, cleaning, laundry, yard maintenance, etc. Live-in. $100 per month."

If one wanted a job like this, one could always get married.

Then there were the socially oriented institutional jobs, like working in a hospital. Unfortunately, I once had a summer job as a nurse's aide when a student. It involved feeding and burping fifty babies during the night shift in a maternity ward. It was a ghastly experience, and undoubtedly induced permanent trauma in the babies.

There were also numerous ads for sales personnel, the only requirement for which is that one be a living human dynamo. These ads usually run like this:

"Dynamic Person. We seek an aggressive success-oriented sales person. If you believe in yourself, come and see us and let us give you the opportunity to prove it! Unparalleled opportunity for the applicant who refuses to accept mediocrity.

$60,000 + Bonus + Car + Expenses."

Unfortunately, I have never had any difficulty accepting mediocrity. I have also always been grateful that we've never had to "sell" anything at the library — our patrons always seem hysterically happy if they're able to find their book.

12

There remained the clerical jobs, some of which required a typing speed of 70 words per minute, plus advanced training on a word processor. Despite an inexhaustible supply of erasable bond, correction fluid, ink eradicator, erasers, etc., I have never been able to type a letter which didn't look as if it had just been recently exhumed. As far as electronic equipment is concerned, I'm still trying to master my 1974 Sony T.V. (As a librarian, however, one can dismiss one's terrible typing as an "unnecessary clerical skill.") However, before the advent of women's liberation which virtually eliminated such blatantly sexist advertising, there used to be another type of job which did not require such advanced training, and was typified in such breezy ads as this:

> **"Gal Friday** needed for friendly, personable office. Cute, outgoing, "personality plus" girl required to work closely with aggresssive manager. No experience necessary."

However, this type of position posed other problems, depending on how deeply one was committed to the A.L.A. **Code of ethics**.

Of course, there always remains the possibility of attracting a sugar daddy. Unfortunately, every man I have ever met seems extremely impressed by the fact that I am employed and is peculiarly loathe to assume an additional financial burden. My father, who is a mine of homely philosophy, once even subtly intimated that "Keeping money in circulation is just about the finest thing a fellow can do in this old life."

Unemployment insurance, anyone?

Why I Hated Library School

Going to library school in the 1950s was a refreshing experience. Like most times of economic affluence, the '50s bred a lofty idealism marked by a total disdain for worldly possessions. However, as some income, however meager, was required to maintain one's sparsely furnished pad, many of us left the exalted realms of liberal arts and succumbed to library school as a last desperate stand to utilize our B.A. However, we didn't succumb willingly. Because we weren't dependent upon faculty recommendations for a job, we lost no opportunity to remind them how stultifying we found the tedious compendium of trivia which constituted their curriculum.

One of our professors, a very sensitive person who had an advanced degree in some arcane subject useful for no other purpose, couldn't seem to stand the regimen himself, and seemed highly sympathetic. His frequent forays against the most hallowed reference tools in American librarianship provided the only real leaven to our course. The **Guide to reference books** by Constance Winchell, who, he assured us, "was almost as big as her book" was, he informed us, extremely useful and could be utilized in two ways: 1) you could sit on it, or 2) you could drop it on the head of some adversary below. He was also fond of extolling the **American people's encyclopedia** as "the encyclopedia for just plain people." Most of the other faculty, however, regarded

14

the curriculum with deadly earnest. One professor, questioned because one of the answers to an exam question did not appear in the text, proclaimed triumphantly, "Aha! Then you **did** miss that footnote on page 459!"

One fascinating aspect of library school was that, although one may do nothing more important than read an article on "How to paste a clipping neatly" or "The status of librarians at Flathead Valley Community College," such activities seemed to take hours to accomplish. It was the source of my greatest frustration that, while a couple of my friends, who were getting an M.A. in an academic subject, constantly criticized the lack of any intellectual content in my studies, they were the ones who had time to spend wild evenings carousing in the city, while I was up till four in the morning preparing an exhaustive bibliography on Armenian religious orders.

As members of the "beat generation", however, we did not openly vent our hostility. We were more discreet, and merely posted unsigned indictments on the bulletin board. The following is a slightly edited and updated version of a satire written by an anonymous, but frustrated, member of our class.

Final Examination — Librarianship 299

1. If you were freezing to death on a desert island which of your library school textbooks would you throw into the fire first?
   a) All of the **Anglo-American cataloguing rules**
   b) Only chapter six of the above.
   c) Other selected chapters. (Please specify)

d) Haines. **Living with books**.

e) McMurtrie. **The book**.

f) Wilson. **The university library**.

2. Fill in the surnames and identify: John, Thomas and Melvil – – – – –

3. Which do you like best?

4. Why?

5. Miss Haines' handwriting has been said to be:

   a) crabby   c) delicate

   b) poorly spaced   d) unreadable

6. The natives of Bora Bora are more critical of television programs than the indigenous population of Kurdistan. True or false?

7. Make a content analysis of the following quotation: "The floor of the library should be strong enough to support the books."

8. Wilson says something about the university library. What does he say?

9-12. State how many bookstores carry a full line of Afghan literature

   a) in the U.S.   c) in Israel

   b) in Swaziland   d) in Afghanistan

13. Discuss the relationship between flying saucers and the medium sized public library.

Do not sign this examination. Statistically it makes no difference.

Some Aspects of Bibliotherapy

The most fascinating thing about public libraries is the vast amount of obsessive research which is conducted there. The innermost dreams and desires which she wouldn't divulge even to her favorite hairdresser, one finds a patron looking up in the card catalog. In fact, if there weren't this opportunity to indulge these secret obsessions, who knows what social havoc would result? If the man who is convinced he owns an original oil painting by Rosa Bonheur couldn't rush in, fiery eyed, at two every afternoon to look under the B's, would he not murder his wife instead? This frantic and unrelenting interest in something beyond oneself gives meaning to life and is a socially accepted outlet for human aggression which might otherwise assume some destructive form.

People vary in their methods of conducting research. One immaculate gentleman comes in every day with an attaché case full of several varieties of pencils, pens, erasers and assorted pads and notebooks which he meticulously places on the table in preparation for his chef-d'oeuvre. He then disappears for half an hour and, on his return, just as meticulously puts them all back and leaves the library. Other people are irrepressible scribblers. One man, over a course of years, systematically transcribed every word ever recorded in our collection about volcanoes. Another inveterate copier — a lady who always brings along a bottle of purified water and holds a Kleenex over her nose — usually chooses a remote corner of the room to do her research (most often behind a filing cabinet) and staff must exercise great care not to stumble over her unawares.

Many people with emotional problems find some brief release by indulging in their own unique type of library research. One young man constantly plays long playing records at sixteen revolutions per minute in an attempt to "crack the secret code." Any record will do, and he is always irritated when told his time in the listening booth is up, because he has "just found the spot." A middle-aged gentleman has now attained complete peace of mind since ascribing his unusual personality to the work of devils. He comes in regularly to look at his "devil book" (a book of reproductions of paintings by Hieronymous Bosch) and chortles by the hour over their antics. One of our most notable patrons was a pyromaniac who had recently escaped from prison. He was suspected of starting a large fire in town, but all the police knew about him, was that he loved Beethoven. Sure enough, as the fire was raging a couple of blocks away, he was discovered in a record booth exulting to the strains of the ninth symphony.

The permissive atmosphere of the library attracts many people who might not feel at home, or would be kicked out, anywhere else. One lady, who, in a supreme attempt at anonymity, wears a fruit crate over her head, comes in between hospitalizations. Another woman wears a boy scout uniform and a yellow yo-yo around her neck, while a faithful gentleman never fails to carry on a non-stop conversation with the third edition of Webster's international dictionary. Other better adjusted patrons, on the other hand, often seem to take up permanent residence. Our most faithful patron in this category, Denny from the O.K. Hotel, was finally interviewed by a local newspaper for his unprecedented feat of sleeping in the same chair for twenty five years.

The daily privilege of observing such a vast and inimitable variety of human beings indulge their obsessions, pursue some brief pleasure or just attempt to maintain their already precarious hold on reality, is one of the greatest pleasures of working in a library.

God in the Library

There is nothing quite so ego-enhancing as believing you're God. It is therefore not surprising that God manifests him/herself every so often in the library.

One of the most remarkable and persistent of our spiritual visitors was Paul Twitchell. Paul systematically read through our entire theological collection to attest its orthodoxy and, as the story goes, assigned to many books his unique "imprimatur" in the form of two rubber stamps. In those books which conformed to his theological views he inserted a slip stamped with a picture of a very benign and beaming little man inscribed "PAUL TWITCHELL APPROVES OF THIS BOOK." Those books which earned his disapprobation, however, contained a slip picturing a very stern and frowning man and the inscription "PAUL TWITCHELL DOES **NOT** APPROVE OF THIS BOOK." It is interesting to note, however, that, although he has since shuffled off this mortal coil, he has recently received his apotheosis in ECKANKAR and, although not considered divine, is believed by his devotees to be dwelling in the "higher planes" from which he communes with his initiates on earth.

God, being rather busy, does not always have time to drop by in person. Sometimes he phones in. One woman, who phoned daily, always asked for the meaning of obscene words. When provided with this information she would exclaim "That's me! I'm the

Great Female [blankety-blank] of the Universe!"

"Yes, madam," the librarian replied politely. "Are there any other words you wish defined? We have other calls coming through."

"That's the trouble nowadays," she groaned. "Nobody wants to hear the truth anymore."

Being God can be a very frustrating occupation, especially if other people aren't willing to acknowledge your divinity. It is therefore not surprising that, in desperation, he is often forced to use the mail. Recently we received a seven page missive, typed single spaced on legal size stationery, outlining His biography, bibliography, manifestations, etc., interspersed with some excerpts from His latest movie reviews. Written in a strange mixture of small and capital letters with frequent letter substitutions (e.g. "B" for "P") it begins "I aM goD....mY BrEsent naMe'S BenEDiCt ScHwartzBerg....onCe EvErY agE i incarnatE in orDEr2SLaY EviL." According to his biography, God has had an interesting and varied career. Born in 1932 in "ConEy ISLanD (aMusEMent Bark)", he obtained a PhD in Classics at Yale, travelled, among other places, to Algiers "wHErE in '59...: EntErED HEavEN & CrEatEd, as nuMBer, the CrEation." After a short manifestation as Buddha he visited San Francisco where he published the announcement "God appeared in Frisco in 1965." After an unsuccessful publishing venture he took a job as a typist in a computer office "tHUS BEginning ManifEstation on citY scaLE." Since then he has revealed his superhuman intelligence but "wHEn BHotograBHic rEcords of

21

THE HigHEst MiraCLEs WErE circuLatEd, ... THE terrified LEadErs&inSTitutions undEr-took a caMBaign of suffocation tHat aiMEd aT BrEvEnting tHE MESSIAH froM coMing, at rEndering ALL His Efforts usELEss..." After a brief outline of His religious principles (e.g., "1st COMMandMEnt:nEvEr Hit Kids, no MattEr wHat") he inserts a revealing biographical note: "after Making THE zEn tEa-cHing scEnE in ManHattan, MovEd Back witH MotHEr at 1773 vYSE AVE., Bronx, tHEn Back to nutHousE in wingdaLE, N.Y." He then proceeds to list his manifestations in which various parts of his body correspond to the geography of New York City, e.g., "MUSTACHE ('MYSTIC'): riBLEY's MEn clo-tHing... TEETH&TONGUE: PEnn-cEntraL raiL-road 'i stick tongue out aLL tHe waY2NEw HavEn')... SEx ORGAN: MiddLE COLLegiatE MEthodist CHurcH ("gordon A. SEaMan organ-ist")" He concludes by offering his services as a typist for $100 a week and by quoting extensively from his works which include an impassioned defense of his grammar: "I AM THE LIGHT ABOUT THE USE OF THE ENGLISH LANGU-AGE IN THIS BOOK ... God does at times fail to respect the often abstruse rules of English gram-mar and ... did change the grammatic rules."

Sex in the Library

It is said that in one small library in the eastern part of the state there is the following entry in the card catalog:

Sex

For sex see librarian.

Although this may indicate an increasing permissiveness among the profession, it is salutary to note that the Library of Congress still upholds the nation's moral standards. Nevertheless, its "see" reference:

Chastity

see

Single women

so infuriated one liberated Ms. on the staff of a large university library, that it was promptly removed from the catalog.

On the job, however, we are the model of decorum. We were therefore understandably indignant when, one day, someone phoned in to ask "Do you have sex in the office?" "Certainly not!" we spluttered, highly conscious of our image and the stringent regulations enforced by City Hall. However, when we realized that she was not actually conducting a survey, but only wanted a book by Helen Gurley Brown, we calmed down somewhat.

Nevertheless, despite the high moral tone set by the staff, sex does play a rather furtive but prominent role for our perennial "peekers." The responses of these men, however, seem fixated at a very preliminary level. As a result, they are rarely dangerous and probably incapable of any normal sexual activity. (The occasional rape is attempted by quite a different personality type.) Anything turns them on, however, and they can spend hours peering over the latest issue of the **Camellia journal** at someone's ankle, while the more advanced may actually prostrate themselves in the aisle for a more intimate glimpse of some housewife, happily browsing through the interior decorating books. Most of the females thus observed are blissfully unaware of the fact, and would be quite shocked that "something like that goes on in the library." In actuality, however, the bookstacks offer a great opportunity to peek, while pretending to be engrossed in more scholarly pursuits. The staff, however, soon recognize such clientele and, because we do not know their real names, call them by some nickname — e.g. "the milkman", "the plastic man", "Banjo eyes", etc.

Until we hired a security guard, much staff time was rather fruitlessly spent trying to discourage their activities. We once asked a peeker, who for some time had been kneeling and peering through book stacks at some high school girls, if he needed any help. He blithely replied, "No, I'm just looking." On another occasion we noticed a particularly adamant peeper poised in front of a long run of the **American art annual**, behind which someone was seated. In an attempt to discourage him, we said "Oh, I don't think these publications would be of much interest to you." "That's what **you** think, lady!" he snorted.

At one time things got so bad that an elite corps of plain-clothes police detectives were called in to clean things up. The most effective of these was a young, attractive, mini-skirted woman who would poise herself seductively at a table in the middle of the room. When she attracted her prey, she would then lure him into the stacks and, and if he made a pass, would promptly arrest him. Her first day on the job claimed several victims, which prompted one staff member to moan "We're losing all our patrons!"

Then, of course, there are other patrons who are interested in just plain sex. One of the most memorable of these was José. On a dull evening he would brighten things up by giving a "toot" on a little brass horn he always carried with him, or would regail us with his wild jazz piano renditions. His main purpose in coming to the library, however, was "to find a woman," an unfortunate predilection which led to his ultimate eviction from the premises. It is interesting to note, however, that the women who objected to his behavior were not those he pro-positioned, but the ones he informed (in no uncertain terms) that they were not quite up to his standards.

One day when he was particularly adamant and the police were called, our evangelistic secretary pursued him into the Newspaper Room in an attempt to convert him.

"I'm just **burning** for a woman! I'm just **burning** for a woman!" he groaned, clutching himself in agony.

"Now, José," she lectured, "this does not come

from the Lord."

"To hell with the Lord."

"It is the Devil who is filling you with these lustful thoughts, José. We all have these feelings which we must learn to control."

"Jeez. With a figure like yours, lady, you've got a man to go to bed with every night."

"Now, José," she continued, "you must forget the body and its evil desires. You must turn to the Lord and be filled with the spirit."

"Yes, I know, lady," he said, somewhat chastened and subdued.

"You should turn all your thoughts to the Lord, José."

"Yes, I know, I know," he said sheepishly. "I should think more about God."

"God will give new purpose and direction to your life."

"Yes, I know. But," he added, with great practicality, "how is all this going to get me a woman?"

The Art Department, or
"How do you make a nativity scene
out of an old ham can?"

With the stock market in its frequent precarious condition, people are turning more and more to art as an investment. Not a week goes by but some excited patron phones up who has just discovered an unsigned painting in the attic which he or she has determined is a Picasso. (In one week we had two Picassos and one Velásquez.) At the other end of the spectrum is the telephone patron who has just found a painting with an unintelligible signature and wants to know "all about the artist." (These paintings are usually untitled nondescript landscapes or rural scenes with multitudinous cows.) Still other patrons specialize in contemporary decorative art (usually owl or barn pictures) which they purchase in department stores. These are usually signed "Smith" or "Brown" while some of the jauntier ones are inscribed with catchy names like "Bobo". To make things worse, patrons also tend to confuse technical precision with genius. One person, who owned a sculpture of a woman (who, she assured us, was "fully clothed"), was extremely frustrated because she could find out nothing about the artist. "But," she exclaimed, "this lady has such **perfect** fingernails — Baglioni **must** be famous!"

Another group of patrons, equally assiduous, yet less commercial, often phone up to identify some painting they saw (or think they saw) years ago in some art museum. Often the scope and detail of these paintings assume rather grandiose proportions with the passage of time. Thus, as much as he insisted upon their existence, we were unable to supply a gentleman with any information on "a magnificient series of murals" by Utrillo entitled "La grande derrière." People are also often fascinated by "what the painter was thinking" when he executed a particular work. This is fairly easy for narrative paintings with well known mythological or religious subjects. It is fairly common for someone to phone up and ask "I have this centaur who is reaching for this naked lady who isn't half a horse. What does it mean?" However, often it is anyone's guess, especially when the query is about some abstract painting titled "Composition no. 89." We were a little surprised, however, when two young men from a local T.V. station asked for "the story behind Washington crossing the Delaware."

"Why, don't you boys know your American history?" we joshed.

"Oh, I remember now, ma'am," one exclaimed brightly. "Wasn't that 'One if by land, two if by sea'?"

However, this does not mean that the spirit of art criticism is dead. One lady, who belongs to a local cultural society, came in to look at reproductions by the British artist, Francis Bacon. She was quite upset when she saw his work, and lamented "how everything has gone downhill since Aristotle." She attributed this to the growing fragmentation of civilization which, she assured us, "was all started by Freud who had this Orpheus complex which made

him think that emotion resided in the genials."
Another patron confided, "I sure like Giotto... I
guess he was quite a religious character. But boy,"
he said wearily, "do I ever get **sick** of his dragons!"

Then, of course, there is the eternal fascination
with the nude, which still exists despite the present
permissive society and the emergence of headier sub-
jects, like erotic art. Still, we were somewhat sur-
prised one day by an elderly gentleman who asked
for a "biography" of Venus.

"Say," he said, "I want to know something about
Venus — about her... you know ... dimensions."
(He waved his hands in the shape of a Coca-Cola
bottle.) "I mean, in them there art magazines ...
there must be some diagrams or something."
However, although we have information on the
Venus de Milo, we could produce no divinely in-
spired statistics. For the record, however, we have
detailed measurements listed under "Venus de Milo
— Dimensions" from which one can extract her
statistics as roughly 51" - 39" - 51".

Related to the art boom is the antiques boom.
Formerly an antique was, by definition, an object
of some aesthetic interest at least one hundred years
old. Now the term is used indiscriminately for any-
thing of any age which anyone has the patience (or
nerve) to accumulate. Usually it is just plain junk
euphemized by such terms as "collectibles" or
"nostalgia items" which many people will go to great
lengths to collect. Not a day goes by but we get a
phone call from someone who exclaims ecstatical-
ly: "My daughter just found the darlingest little thing
in the garbage dump! He's the cutest little guy in

short pants sitting on a tree stump with a tennis racket under his arm. Do you know anything about it?'' Such items are usually difficult to document.

As the newer collectibles become established and prices for depression glass, left handed mustache cups and Mason jars rise to unprecedented heights, collectors turn to ever more ingenious and unexploited items. At times these have included brothel tokens, Planter Peanut collectibles, barbed wire and animal traps. Often, however, by the time a meticulous price guide for such items is compiled, the mania has subsided and people are already collecting something else.

Because of the rise in prices, people in dire need of capital are selling their treasured possessions while others are acquiring more as a hedge against inflation. We didn't realize that things were quite so bad, however, until a patron phoned to ask about the value of an 1889 gold piece. Visibly disappointed that it wasn't worth more, she sighed with great resignation, ''Well, I guess I won't dig up my grandmother after all. She was buried with two in her coffin.''

On the Love of Books

One of the things which is supposed to redeem librarians in the public image is that, however crabby and formidable we may seem, we have a great "love of books." In fact, I once met a student who confessed, very humbly and abjectly, that he didn't think he could ever "aspire" to be a librarian because he "didn't love books enough."

This love of books is supposed to be as impartial as it is passionate — it is supposed to be an all-inclusive, all-consuming obsession which embraces everything in sight — in or out of print — regardless of author or title. I once actually worked for someone who possessed this universal love for books. At the end of a twelve hour day she would totter home under a load of volumes ranging from **Some igneous rocks of lower Matebeland** to **The meaning of the wild strawberry in medieval French literature** — all of which she intended to "browse" through before going to bed. (The ultimate affront to this universal type of book lover would be the suggestion that one might actually sit down and "read" one of them.) When I finally had an opportunity to examine the contents of her personal library, I discovered it contained a small nucleus of English girl detective stories circa 1910.

The truth is that (at least judging from staff book orders) the literary level of many librarians is not particularly high. Whether or not the frustrations induced by working eight hours a day are incompat-

31

ible with Proust, the fact remains that many staff members prefer to read something more practical like **Ninety-two creative new ways to prepare an avocado** or **How to live with your pet schnauzer**. (We even once had a staff order for Master and Johnson's **Human sexual response** to which was attached the enigmatic note "Cancel if received after June 1969.") After the trauma of the day, one harrassed department head I know actually finds it relaxing to read a horror story before going to bed.

Frankly, I dislike most books. Most of them are not worth the paper they are printed on. The practical ones will date in ten years and of those that comprise "literature" only a fraction of one percent will be recognized in one hundred years.

Yet, even this small percentage is formidable. If one is working forty hours a week, the only solution is to read selectively, restricting oneself to works of genius. At breakfast you can always get in a few lines of **The rise and fall of the Roman empire** while buttering your toast. The Bible is particularly recommended at lunch — especially big Bibles. People will avoid you like the plague, thus ensuring you a nice quiet spot to yourself, and the waitress, awed by your spirituality, will accept a smaller tip. **War and peace** will see you through many a coffee break and the **Bhagavad Gita**, arranged as it is in small meditative units, is ideal for the bathroom. If one reads slowly and with discernment, this list alone should occupy anyone for at least ten years. With a little insight one can soon compile a significant bibliography to last one for life and, by exercising a little judgment, still avoid reading **The critique of pure reason**.

The Literature Department, or
"Is King Lear in the Old or New Testament?"

One of the most delicate duties in a literature department is recommending novels for recreational reading, none of which ever have been nor ever will be enshrined in world literature. When the patron has asked the inevitable "Have you got anything good today?" one must, through a series of discreet questions, ascertain the exact degree of sex or violence desired so that one neither offends nor disappoints the reader. These novels run the gamut from the "wholesome" (100% pure) to the "sophisticated" (slightly sexy) to the "frank" (downright pornographic). (One might as well forget about the latter as they are never in.) Taste varies a great deal in this type of reading. As someone I know puts it "I don't mind 'in and out of bed' every twenty pages or so, but I don't like 'in and out of bed' every other page." Some people, however, will accept a little libido if the novel has a compensating religious theme. As one sweet older lady confided, when she brought back **David and Bathsheba**, "I wouldn't have read that if it hadn't been based on the Bible. . . . My, they were rascals!" One lady, however, stated very adamantly that she wanted "a nice adventure story" — but "nothing with lust in it" — as she worked in a home for unwed mothers.

People often have very precise requirements for the type of novel they wish to read. One lady refused to read any novels which had smoking in them as it was "a filthy habit." (A bibliography of such novels undoubtedly exists, but was not readily available at the time.) Another woman wanted books of sad short stories, as she had heard that weeping clears the sinuses.

Then, of course, there is the constant demand for literary criticism. Some of these scholars, like high school students, do their research only under duress. Normally they refuse to do a report on any item over thirty pages. One young man, however, tired of this superficial approach, announced, "I have to do a report on **The tale of two cities** and intend to go into it pretty deeply — Do you have **Masterplots**?"

There is, however, a hard core of patrons who become quite obsessed about literary allusions and spend much time engrossed in their explication. One lady phones in promptly at nine o'clock every morning to ask about all the difficult words and figures of speech she has encountered in the newspaper the night before. One week she phoned several times a day about the use of the word "albatross." The staff patiently repeated the literal meaning, the literary allusion and the symbolic uses of the word each time. By the end of the week she called again, the explanation of the word having crystallized into two distinct possibilities. The newspaper, she explained, had said that Lyndon Johnson went to his grave with the albatross of the war in Vietnam around his neck. She now knew that this mean that he was buried with either 1) an aquatic bird, or 2) an English poet named Coolidge. Neither seemed particularly strange to her; she just wanted to know which it was.

Sometimes, however, our resources are just not

adequate to deal with some patrons' research — e.g. the lady tracing Hamlet's genealogy to prove that Hamlet's mother was married three times: first to Hamlet's father, then to his uncle, and then to Macbeth. Some patrons, when supplied with an answer, are still not content. One person, who asked a staff member to translate a motto into classical Greek, given the translation, exclaimed, "I just love it, but haven't you got something shorter?"

Then, of course, there is the indomitable bevy of patrons who, not content to read the books of others, wish to produce their own. These are a very assiduous breed who are absolutely compulsive, not so much about the nuances of characterization, as about the details of physical description in their work. One girl, who was writing a Christmas story, wished to know if the road between Nazareth and Bethlehem was paved at the time of the Nativity. (Unfortunately we were unable to produce any pertinent Roman engineering records in this connection.) Another lady called to find out what kind of bathtubs the Plaza Hotel in New York City used in 1932. She was writing her autobiography and wished to be extremely factual when recalling the time she got stuck in one of them. The librarian tactfully suggested that she describe the tub as "very narrow" and let it go at that, which seemed to satisfy her request.

On Religiosity in Libraries

It appears to be a natural tendency in human beings to glorify their occupation (and, therefore, themselves) far out of proportion to its actual nature. This is, of course, the psychology behind calling garbage collectors "sanitation engineers" and janitors "building superintendents." Rather than accepting a job on its own terms and executing it with dignity, there seems to be a necessity to provide it with a glamorous rhetoric and mystique which it does not possess.

It is interesting to note that, among those whose professions are by nature idealistic — e.g., doctors and clergymen — there seems to be no desire to change the terminology of their work. So far, there does also not appear to be a movement to change the name "librarian", but, within the ranks of librarianship — perhaps because of the quiet, unobtrusive nature of our work — there has always been a desire to describe our activities in terms of heroism, self-sacrifice and religious consecration. There seems to be an attempt to invest librarianship with an inherent drama it does not possess. I remember seeing a recruitment film in the late '50s sponsored by the Canadian Library Association in which, in order to portray the heightened excitement and adventure of working in a cataloging department, the music (a tumultuous work by Tchaikovsky) rose to a climactic frenzy as the cataloger finally located the correct L.C. subject heading.

Such library fantasies are not restricted to propaganda films alone, however, but are perpetuated in library schools and library literature — mostly by people remote from the frustrating everyday reality of the work in which we are involved. I endured library school in order to have a pleasant, absorbing occupation — not to become a saint. Much to my surprise, I heard the organizer of the first Contra Costa County bookmobile compared favorably to, if not to the actual disadvantage of, the early Franciscan missionaries — and wondered what I was getting into. Similarly, I found reference librarians extolled as the "last of the universal men", although I realized that, with a forty hour work week, I would have little time to read much more than the **Reader's digest**.

Similarly, library literature seems to divide itself between the very technical or the very inspirational articles. Thus, if one does not care to read about a statistical analysis of the circulation records at Podunk Junior College, one can always turn to S.R. Ranganathan — that guru of library literature — who has injected a note of oriental transcendentalism into his work. In his book **Reference service**, next to a chapter called "Difficult reference librarian", he has included one entitled "Mystic picture of reference service", which includes subdivisions like "Light from the Vedas", etc., all of which are accompanied by liberal quotations in Sanskrit.

Librarianship is also not without its religious relics. A friend of mine reports visiting the Columbia University Library where the guide reverently showed them "Miss Winchell's chair" which was carefully roped off for the veneration of the devout. It was apparently very decorously designed to befit the dignity of its occupant, and no one else on the staff presumed to sit in it.

Although I didn't mind putting up with a few euphemisms in library school, I was quite unprepared to encounter it in my first job. Unfortunately, however, our department head proved to be the living incarnation of all the sacred ideals we had learned about. Due to some physical malfunction, she only required four hours sleep, the remaining twenty hours of which she spent in her office talking simultaneously on two telephones. Her spare time was devoted to the pursuit of knowledge. During lunch hours she attended a lecture or a poetry reading. (She gave up the latter, however, after hearing a poem about an unfulfilled librarian, which she considered totally irrelevant, as the author was only a part time clerk and therefore lacked the necessary professional insight.) Every fall she signed up for several extension courses, enrolling nine consecutive times in Russian, which she always dropped after the second lecture when the exotic excitement of learning a foreign language yielded to the dreary realities of grammar.

Working for this woman was like entering a religious order where one was expected to observe all three monastic vows (except, of course, that of poverty). If one did not show the appropriate fervor, one was correspondingly reprimanded. A rigid monastic discipline prevailed. Physical functions were to be carefully coordinated so that one only went to the bathroom during one's coffee break.

Strangely enough, however, some vocations actually flourished under so many rigid restrictions. One of this woman's former employees who went on to gain Fame in the Library World actually referred to her affectionately as her "Library Mother." The rest of us, however, disappeared miraculously at 5:00 p.m. Some who had cars, however, might linger a moment or two longer, as she always emerged from her office at five after five to exclaim incredulously, "Where is everybody?"

Needless to say, such days of repression are over. The woman has long since retired and, the last I heard, had just enrolled in a hat making course and was preparing to take her sixth trip to South America. I have had the privilege of working for dedicated people since, but, although they seemed to appreciate a conscientious day's work from their employees, they have all been quiet and unassuming and would never presume to impose some ridiculous heroic ideal from above. They have all been able to distinguish between religion and librarianship.

Since then, I have not been confronted with expositions of library sanctity except during after-dinner speeches at convention banquets. However, with careful precautions, one can usually attain a state of happy oblivion beforehand, during which one does not hear the speech at all, or, if one is "compos mentis", can, for a few brief moments, actually believe it.

The Technology Department, or
"What is the gestation period of the elephant?"

Compared to the sometimes rarified atmosphere of other departments, Techology offers a refreshing change. It is the gutsy "how to do it" department where the harrassed housewife can run in for a recipe for geoduck before rushing home to rescue her roast from the oven, or a man can pick up a repair manual to fix the transmission on his '49 Ford. These patrons do not usually have the leisure nor the temperament to spend all day engrossed in arcane research, but come in for some quick piece of practical information before the five minutes on their parking meter runs out.

It is amazing the number of people who, not content with commercial products or services, wish to "do it themselves." These people think nothing of devoting entire weekends to learn **25 new ways to clip your poodle**, while the number of doghouses under construction alone in this country boggles the imagination. Although the latter may seem to be a fairly simple form of architecture, its builders impose extremely demanding aesthetic standards, and, although one may drag out eighteen different plans from various sources, it's never the "right" doghouse.

Another favorite subject for do-it-yourselfers is the whole field of medicine. For this reason, although most libraries buy the inspirational "how to live with your ingrown toenails" type of book, they avoid buying medical textbooks for fear that the patron, if he knows too much, may attempt major surgery in the kitchen. (Despite this, one of our patrons proudly related how he successfully cut out a cyst from his wrist with the aid of the **Merck manual**.)

One interesting phenomenon in this department is the way many people become totally engrossed by some disease they have contracted, real or imaginary. Instead of regarding this as something negative, it seems to give many a new lease on life and an obsessive, all-consuming interest which they formerly never possessed. They never tire of reading of its symptoms and every detail of its ultimate progression, while those with some equally serious, but extremely rare, disease, consider themselves particularly privileged.

This obsession with dying is probably also responsible for the strange fascination aroused by mortuary science, a field in which, perhaps, more books are stolen than any other. It exerts a particular fascination for young teen-age girls who are always writing job studies about it and almost always want ''a few pictures of embalming'' to brighten up their essay.

Although their condition is rarely fatal, pregnant mothers are equally obsessed by their state. They wish to observe their progress day by day, and, although their curiosity is understandable, it results in a great problem with overdue books, most of which are not returned until nine months later.

Interest in all sorts of women's problems is also rampant. Although these do not seem to phase the younger men in the department, who can discuss the

41

fine points of breast self-examination with great insouciance, it does bother certain middle-aged men who wish that "some of those ladies wouldn't ask some of those questions" and look desperately around for some female librarian with whom they can exchange a question on refrigerator repair.

"Do-it-yourselfers," however, do not necessarily restrict themselves to legal activities. Every once in a while some rather suspect looking character will come in looking for "books on locks and keys and explosives." The drug culture is also in evidence. Some of these people quite openly ask for **The marijuana pot grower's handbook** while others, more reticent, but obviously interested in making heroin, ask for "books on oriental flowers." The tendency to grow marijuana under lights has also severely reduced our supply of indoor light gardening books.

Such departments usually boast one or two "researchy" types who have their own obsessions. There is always some librarian who can either completely reassemble a model T Ford or who has sublimated his life in the U.S. Patent Office **Official gazette**. One of the latter, a middle-aged bachelor who never cooks, has his stove and refrigerator stuffed with old shoe boxes full of esoteric indexes to patents, including a mysterious one devoted to lady inventors, the source of which he has never divulged.

However, even such master researchers cannot always satisfy a patron's demands. One of these gentlemen once had a lady on the phone who wanted a great deal of information on the construction of a local bridge. When he explained to her that it would take him a little time to get all the material together, she became quite irate and exclaimed, "Why, don't you have a Xerox machine down there? I saw one like it at the World's Fair, and I know — you just press a button and all the information comes out in a couple of minutes!"

On Neuroticism in Libraries

There has always been a screening process in library schools which seems to favor the young, robust, sociocentric, outgoing person in an effort to "upgrade" the image of librarians, and to reject the withdrawn neurotic applicant who would only perpetuate the unattractive image we are said to possess. This screening process was in effect when I applied as well. Indeed, one of my professors, whose vacation was ruined by having to fill out countless questionnaires in quadruplicate to accompany my effusive essay on "Why I want to go to Library School", was led to exclaim "It seems harder to get you into library school than to get someone out of Alcatraz."

In the end, however, because there was a labor shortage and there weren't many of us depression babies on the market, everyone was accepted. However, instead of the effusive personality types the faculty may have anticipated, they were stuck with all of us hopeless neurotics. In our class alone there was at least one aspiring artist, two or three frustrated actors, an irascible Egyptologist and (what the rest of us considered the acme of maladjustment) — someone who actually studied library science until four in the morning. Most of the rest of us were recovering from some traumatic experience in teaching. Only one or two fitted the "glamour girl" image which was so popular at the time, and those have probably long since left the Library World to become successful society matrons.

Although most of us were able to successfully preserve our neuroses in Library School — in some cases actually enhance them — it is unfortunate that such discrimination exists. Melvil Dewey hardly strikes one as a "normal" person. And, who knows what secrets lurked within the soul of L. Quincy Mumford? On a more universal level one doesn't have to read many biographies of genii to realize that the impetus to their creativity lay in some unresolved emotional conflict which was sublimated into religion or art. It may have been St. Paul's sexual hangup which enabled him to write his great paean to Christian love. Beethoven was a complete nut who exasperated everyone, yet whose infinite self-pity and longing for affection found release in his music.

One is referring here, of course, to sublimated neurotics. (Just being neurotic is not enough. It merely makes one crabby — or, even worse — socially destructive.) Anyone in their right mind, of course, would prefer to find fulfillment in their immediate personal relationships. But this is not possible for everyone. People who have felt deprived of affection from their earliest childhood must find other methods of fulfillment. Through sublimation one is often able to channel such painful feelings into some fruitful and positive activity with a greater direction and purpose than is possible for people who find satisfaction in close family relationships. If this sublimation is successful, it can remove the negative elements of the neurosis so that, for all practical purposes, the person's behavior is, in all other respects, normal.

I once knew a tormented neurotic musical genius who was in such a perpetual state of crisis that none of us thought he would ever survive the school year. To our great surprise, however, although he was wild and turbulent two weeks before, he returned from the semester break possessing a strange and impenetrable inner calm.

"What on earth happened?" we asked. "You look half normal."

"Oh," he replied nonchalantly, "I was just playing the piano."

He then went on to explain how this process took place, describing with great lyricism the structure of a symphony in which there are conflicting themes which are eventually resolved. Music had the same effect upon his personality by reconciling his inner conflicts and creating a profound harmony within him. It is through this process of "resolution" that such sublimation occurs.

As in other fields of human endeavor, the unusual productivity of many librarians may well be the result of such sublimation. The extremely well adjusted person, only too eager to rush home to the bosom of his or her family at 5:30, might yawn and reply, when asked a difficult question, "Have you tried the catalog?" The neurotic librarian, however, will immediately become tense and alert — rush to the catalog to track down all available resources, check all existing periodical indexes and other special files, then, if all else fails, take the patron's name and phone number, and pursue the answer with an indefatigable bird dog mentality long after everyone else has left. Such people may not be "normal" but they are excellent librarians and a great asset to society.

No doubt most of us fall between the poles of the super well adjusted blob who is just putting in time and the hyper-energetic Stakhanovite worker who is totally committed to his or her job. Nevertheless, I find it difficult not to sympathize with a sign I once saw in front of a hippy pad proclaiming "Fight mental health."

Neurotics of the Library World arise! You have nothing to lose but normality.

The Education and Sociology Department, or "Do you have a civil service exam for call girls?"

Perhaps it is the humdrum lives most of us lead that has resulted in the phenomenal growth of interest in the occult in the past few years. There seems to be an almost universal desire to attribute to some dramatic supernatural or extraterrestrial force phenomena which we do not, or prefer not, to understand. At any rate, being "on line" with a Martian is infinitely more exciting than talking to one's husband, and satisfies a need for some sort of fantasy world which most us seem to require.

One patron, who was obsessed with the flying saucers she had seen "come down from the mountains" hoped we would use our contact with the public to tell everyone, so that the F.B.I. would finally do something. "If," she stated, "the F.B.I. would stop wasting their money looking for that 'Indomitable Snowman' and start a saucer search, all would not be lost." She had informed this agency accordingly, but they just "hollered and pounded on the desk — they think they know everything." (As she left she advised us to use Aztec arithmetic to compute the household budget. If the rest of the family get nosey, they'll never figure it out.)

Witchcraft is still popular, and many covens exist, most of which, according to statistics, are devoted to black magic. During its heyday occasionally a whole coven would descend upon us at once, which prompted one staff member to remark

48

rather wearily, "Why can't they just live lives of quiet desperation like the rest of us?" Some patrons, however, are more casual in their approach and "just want to cast a few spells."

Astrology, however, always attracts a steady clientele, although the result of the research may be disillusioning. It seems to attract people who hope to discover some hitherto unsuspected but infinitely flattering facet of their own personality. Before we were able to obtain the more positive sounding books on oriental astrology and had to refer to books on Far Eastern symbolism, we hated to tell one lady, who was fascinated by the fact that she was born in "the year of the monkey," that "the money . . . is commonly regarded as the emblem of ugliness and trickery." Another caller, wishing to paint posters of her friends' zodiac signs, asked what color was associated with Virgo. She was not particularly happy when informed that it was "black with blue splotches."

The ones who are really "into" this subject, however, spend hours compiling special astrological charts, usually of their favorite movie star, which they send to him/her free of charge. For this purpose they require the latitude, longitude and time zone of the person's place of birth. This is not in itself particularly difficult unless, as is commonly the case, you have to establish whether it was Daylight or Standard time in Goose Lake, Iowa on Sept. 9, 1916.

Then there is the vast clientele for the plethora of self-improvement books with titles like **How to become the new, magnetic, magnificent you in four-**

teen days instead of the slob everyone thinks you are. Judging from the popularity of this type of literature a large proportion of the population must be riddled with self doubts and anxiety. One patron who reserved a book in this genre was notified by phone that it was missing and therefore no longer available. Unfortunately, his wife took the message and, being rather curious, asked what her husband had requested. We were obliged to inform her that the title was **How to live with a neurotic**.

As this department contains the books on love and marriage, it attracts a large number of patrons who wish to form romantic attachments. Some patrons use the direct approach and insert a slip in the card catalog reading "If you want a date call 872-6311 — any time." Others, however, prefer the more formal bibliographical approach. One gentleman over fifty with very high moral standards wished a list of agencies through which he could contact a "young, clean-living, non-smoking, non-drinking single female" who would not object to the fact that he was already married. Another eager patron, a teen-age girl, wished to consult "the list of all unmarried men." As this book was not immediately identifiable, she explained, rather impatiently, "You know — if you start dating a guy you can look him up and make sure he isn't married already. **All** libraries have it."

Melvil Dewey inserted a small place in his classification scheme for women in 396, between "Etiquette" (395) and "Gypsies. Nomads. Outcast races" (397). An interesting change in the attitude of women — from a passive acceptance of their lot to more aggressive pursuit — can be traced through titles in this category, ranging from **300 things a bright girl can do** (1903), **Books of interest and consolation to spinsters** (1904), **Live alone and like it, a guide for the extra woman** (1937), to current more explicit titles like **The sensuous divorcée**.

Patrons interested in women's literature range all the way from the rather simpering devotees of **Fascinating womanhood** to the more rabid disciples of Gloria Steinem. One of the latter, a sensible middle-aged housewife before she discovered women's lib, suddenly let down her long gray hair and blossomed forth in a poncho and shocking pink hot pants. This movement had inspired her to devote all her energies to protest the new international graphic symbol on women's restrooms which depicts a woman wearing a skirt. "And," she exclaimed in horror, "it's going to be accepted by **twenty-eight** countries!" (Explicit anatomical drawings, anyone?)

An occasional male also wanders into this section, drawn by the fascinating mystery of the female psyche. On one occasion a highly overwrought young man came in to find a book on "how girls go about getting a husband." He explained, with some trepidation, that he was determined never to get married and needed to be prepared for all possible contingencies.

The Classification Survey

A classification survey was recently conducted in our library during the course of which each staff member had to write a short analysis of his or her job. Because the results of this study would inevitably affect the status and salary of our positions, it is only to be expected that certain typical responses emerged from the staff.

The first of these was the self-aggrandizing response, typical of the employee who fears that his or her position will be underrated. These summaries read something like this:

"The purpose of my position is to locate information for the patron from the many faceted bibliographical resources and other sophisticated data bases in our department. Besides my total commitment to the profession for which I am recognized everywhere, my invaluable experience and unique subject expertise acquired through many years of indefatigable study, reading and social involvement have enabled me to offer unexcelled service in person, by correspondence or by telephone. My brilliance of intellect, however, is even exceeded by the charm and magnetism of my personality which never fails to establish immediate rapport with the patron. It is, in fact, people like myself whose unique and indispensable gifts have exalted American librarianship to the level of prestige and excellence it now enjoys throughout the world."

The second response was the use of a certain literary style which could only have been inspired by the dense and rather abstruse survey report conducted a year or two before in our library. Despite its unintelligibility, its inimitable style appears to have been contagious. Many replies were written in library survey-ese, and read something like this: (translations are supplied)

1. List in a series of brief statements the accountabilities of your position:
   a) "Instituting cost effective mechanisms by applying a pre-determined methodology for the maximum utilization of library resources." (I write on the back of old bus transfers.)
   b) "Prioritizing professional activities to accommodate interaction of departmental segments for the ultimate maximization of service delivery." (I let the page look for the missing issue of **Just buttons**.)

2. Specifically describe the part of your job that presents the greatest mental demands on you.
   a) $Y = C_0 + C_7 X_7 + C_2 X_2 + \ldots C_n X_n$
   b) "Developing potentially dynamic and creative interrelationships with patrons who lack the necessary alphabeto-numeric skills to locate multiple digit numbers posted in logical sequence." (If they're too dumb to find their book, that's their tough luck.)

3. What kind of training, education, etc., do you feel your successor should have?
   "I know nothing whatever about my job, but

possess several advanced degrees in business administration. Besides, I believe the patrons should develop more decisive help/self-help strategies in accessing information retrieval systems." (I tell them to look it up in the catalog.)

The Music Department, or,
"What were they singing when they went down on the Titanic?"

One of the most popular pastimes of music patrons is trying to identify some old half forgotten song. And, like the person who is looking for "that little blue book" he saw on the shelf last week, they can often not supply much more pertinent information. Frequently all they can remember is a couple of words from a middle line, or, like one young girl who wanted to identify a song once sung by Mario Lanza, can only recall "It's a kind of love type thing." Often, however, they can remember a fragment of the melody which they chortle gleefully into your ear. "It does 'dum de dum'" they sing, reassuringly. Other times they can remember the song title and you soon find yourself singing a couple of lusty choruses of the Notre Dame football song over the phone.

Of all the recordings in the audio collection, the foreign language records are among the most popular. Many of these patrons already appear to be multi-lingual, having mastered seven or nine languages. It is not uncommon, for example, to hear one of these linguists say "I learned Mandarin last week. Do you have anything in advanced Russian?" Others, however, like one nostalgic army veteran who requested a record on "Tugalug", lamented his lack of language expertise. "You see, I was with General MacArthur in the Second World War and

I met this here girl I wanted to marry in the Philippines. But she didn't speak no English and I didn't know no Tugalug." Now that he was retired, he was determined to make up for lost time.

Music record patrons, however, are often much fussier about their selections. Not only must they have the right arrangement of the music they seek, but they are even sometimes offended by the record jacket. One young girl who wanted the music from the film "Doctor Zhivago" was horrified when she saw the record cover. "**Kiss**-ing!" she screeched. "Ugh! Yuuk! Goo-**ey**! I don't want **that**!"

One of the hazards of working in a music department is the constant cacophony of sound one is subjected to. One whole hour of uninterrupted frog croaks or whale sounds emanating from a record booth is about all anyone can stand, while, during Halloween, the constant turmoil of howling winds, clanking chains and terrifying shrieks (listed in the catalog under "wierd music") seems to portend imminent departmental disaster. Such sound effects records are particularly popular with the public, although some of those requested may be difficult to locate — e.g., the sound of a rhesus monkey getting an inoculation or that of a frog coming out of a pond.

The piano room also attracts its devotees, including a self-confessed "alcoholic piano player" who had formerly only found this instrument in saloons. Its clientele are a loyal lot, some coming in daily to perform. One gentleman, whose pièce de résistance consists of "Tip-toe thru' the tulips", which he plays for hours in a maddening "plunketyplunk" style, so irritated everyone, that one of the staff finally checked out this piece of music, so that, at least for a month, he was forced to expand his repertoire. Then there is the patron who, at 4:30 p.m., in the depths of the afternoon when one's morale is at its lowest ebb, comes in like clockwork to play a doleful rendition of what can only be described as the "concerto morbido."

Music, like the other arts, inspires a host of local creative talent. Aside from a few songs in the fairy genre like "There are trolls trippling through my garden" or "Henry Frost, brother of Jack", most of these song writers seem impelled to write impassioned and effusive lyrics about their own home town. These songs, with titles like "I'd fight a battle to get back to Seattle" or "My heart belongs to Sequim" usually go something like this:

Enumclaw, I hear you calling!
Other cities are appalling.
How could I ever leave you
Where the girls are so darned true blue
For some cold and distant clime
Where they don't know how to give you
   a good time?
Enumclaw, for you I pine.
But soon I'll be home,
No longer to roam,
Back to that good old Puget Sound home
   sweet home of mine.

On Pickled Patrons

Ever since the American Library Association was formed in 1876 under the heroic motto, "Bringing books and people together," a mythology of public librarianship has evolved which, in reality, bears little resemblance to the actual nature of our work. These illusions were encouraged by Andrew Carnegie who envisioned hoards of earnest, industrious workers flocking to their local library after the completion of a sixty hour work week, in search of self education and enlightenment.

The first of these misconceptions, which the A.L.A. has made no attempt to dispel, is that our patrons are absolutely normal. One can enjoy the outrageous humanity of some nut out on the street, but as soon as he enters the library one is supposed to repress all normal criteria of human judgment and regard him with rapt veneration — like some pickled religious relic — however bizarre his request. This is not to suggest that every human being should not be treated with dignity or that every attempt should not be made to answer his question, but that, somehow, silently, in the depths of our being, we should at least be able to accept him for what he is — another magnificent aberration of mankind — rather than striving to maintain some ludicrous professional illusion of what he is not.

The second myth is that our patrons are constantly striving onward and upward to reach higher and even more ineffable echelons of enlightenment. This, of course, is a patent untruth. In almost ten years of public librarianship I have only met one patron who was seeking enlightenment and he was, by his own admission, insane. In fact, some patrons actively oppose any attempt to enlighten them. One such patron became extremely agitated when told that the books on poker he was looking for were in the Education Department. "Oh, I don't want no education, ma'am!" he exclaimed, aghast with fright. "I just want to play poker." It took great reassurance on our part to convince him that the good people in that department would not force an education on him, but merely show him a good book on poker.

Most patrons come in to do their own highly individual and offbeat research, which, although very beneficial to their mental health — a fact which in itself justifies the existence of public libraries — in no way approaches the sublime intent Mr. Carnegie had in mind. (We once had a patron who was intensely preoccupied with embroidering burlap bags. This activity, along with its inherent problem of whether or not to put on a pom pom, kept his mind from being obsessed by the thought of death.) In our department, for example, we would like to give the impression that most patrons are trying to identify some rare Chagall lithograph, but this is hardly the case. In fact, one afternoon, simultaneously, one librarian was deeply involved in teddy-bear research, another was trying to find out who painted "Boy with a bunny", while a third was trying to ascertain the botanical name for "fluffy ruffles." However, despite the proven social value of such research, some librarians are reluctant to admit they spend all day doing this sort of thing.

There seems to be a gap between our honest acknowledgement in private of what we do and the sublime image of our work which we wish to present to the public. For, although we may delight to regale ourselves at coffee breaks with stories about our favorite patrons or questions, as soon as such stories are committed to print, someone arises within the ranks to accuse us of "putting down the patrons." The truth is, however, that our patrons have no such preconceived or exalted idea of how they should act. They are uniquely and exuberantly themselves and refuse to conform to some rigid standard imposed by a profession which, officially at least, seems reluctant to admit that, in reality, it is rarely attained.

It appears that the more highly educated a professional group becomes, the more it overidealizes itself and its work. It is not surprising, therefore, that the members of COYOTE have a far more realistic attitude to their patrons than, correspondingly, do some members of the A.L.A.

Boo-Boos

Young girl, yawning, "My mother's down in geometry — she's traced **some**body back to 800."

###

"I want the Ernest Hemingway translation of Omar Khayyám."

###

First fifth grader: "What does she mean by Fiction and Non-fiction?"
Second fifth grader: "Aw, use your head. What does it sound like? Fiction has a fixed place on the shelves and Non-fiction she puts where she wants.

###

"Do you have the book **Robinson Krushchev?**"

###

"We don't usually come into the main library. We generally use the Oldsmobile."

###

"My daughter needs **The progressive pilgrim** by Paul Bunyan."

###

"You got **Alabama and the forty thieves?**"

###

"Do you have **Abalone and the 4000 thieves?**"

A lady called in to ask the location of Boys' Town. "You know — where they rejuvenate boys."

###

"I want to look up some magazine articles. Where do you keep your index to prodigal literature?"

###

Two young boys asked for the **Hunchback of Notre Dame**.
"Do you know what it's about?" the librarian asked.
"Sure, it's a football story, isn't it?"

###

"What is the term used for pregnancy in the Utopian tubes?"

###

"Do you have something by that French author, Bête Noir?"

###

"I'd like to read up on the Abdominal Snowman."

###

"I would like something on the Bible — I think it's non-fiction."

###

"Do you use the Dewey Dismal Classification?"

###

On Gaining Immortality in Libraries

Although one often hears of someone who has "gone on to gain fame in the Library World", such "fame" is, at best, elusive. It usually means that such a person may be known to a handful of other librarians, but scarcely to the world at large. It rarely results in having one's picture on the cover of **Time** or being interviewed on a late night talk show.

There have been some librarians in the past, however, like Casanova or Leibniz, whose fame has transcended the rather narrow boundaries of our profession. These have been primarily writers who have been connected with well known European libraries.

One of these, Gotthold Ephraim Lessing, an eighteenth century German dramatist, whose works I was forced to read as an undergraduate, was librarian at the Herzogliche Bibliothek at Wolffenbüttel. As an act of retribution, I decided to discover exactly what he contributed to the history of library science. Extensive research, however, reveals that he seems to have done very little. I can find no reference to the fact that he ever cataloged a book or answered a reference question. There is certainly no historical evidence to suggest that he ever spent all day looking for the name of Zorro's horse. His job was, in fact, a sinecure. He was a kind of "librarian in residence" who maintained a drafty study in which he spent all day eeking out his rather tedious classical dramas and avoiding the patrons as much as possible. In fact, in an essay describing his library's collection, he states that he has deliberately avoided publishing a list of its contents "as it would only arouse much trivial and unnecessary speculation and be a source of great personal inconvenience to myself."

Times have changed, however. With the development of library service, even the Librarian of Congress is expected to put in an eight hour day, and there is little opportunity to exercise one's histrionic talents on staff time. In fact, as far as "fame" is concerned, there are few professions where the public pays as little attention to you. To the patrons we are simply bodies who emerge from the woodwork to show them the latest book on Donald Duck collectibles and, as far as they are concerned, are completely devoid of any distinguishing characteristics of age, sex or other personal attributes. This is very comforting to those of us who enjoy such anonymity and do not aspire to be "big personalities" (indeed, such theatrical types are usually more attracted to teaching), but can be very confusing if a patron returns for further help. One of our patrons, who was completely sublimated in his nineteenth century cow picture, was totally baffled when asked to describe the physical characteristics of the librarian who had previously helped him. When, after exhausting all other possibilities, we asked if she were pregnant, he because quite upset. "Oh, m'am!" he exclaimed in agony. "I didn't notice anything like that!"

Thus, as our public pay so little attention to us, the only way we can make any permanent impact on posterity is by the records we leave behind — our catalog cards and index files. Although it may seem strange to a non-cataloger, cataloging is a very subjective process. Each librarian has his or her inimitable style which can be instantly recognized by anyone familiar with their work.

Our own information index, for example, is a hotbed of revealing personality characteristics — a complete "who's who" of the generations of staff who have contributed to it. On leafing through it one can say "This is the brilliant librarian whose impeccable style and logical subject headings are the model on which it is based"; "This is so-and-so, the astute but indefatigable indexer — only **she** would think of indexing a picture of St. Fina of Tuscany"; or, "This is the dum-dum who wrote inspirational essays instead of concise annotations," etc. And, as one recedes into the mists of time, one becomes increasingly fascinated by the crabbed handwriting on ugly brown stock documenting multitudinous references to pictures of tearooms and griffins — the "hot" subjects of their day — and cannot help but marvel that such ancient personalities, so prominent in the formation of our collection, still endure.

4/08
9/10
9/97 4/17